Baby Zebras at the Zoo

Eustacia Moldovo

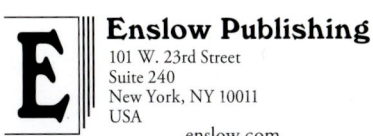
Enslow Publishing
101 W. 23rd Street
Suite 240
New York, NY 10011
USA
enslow.com

Published in 2016 by Enslow Publishing, LLC.
101 W. 23rd Street, Suite 240, New York, NY 10011

Copyright © 2016 by Enslow Publishing, LLC.
All rights reserved.

No part of this book may be reproduced by any means without the written permission of the publisher.

Library of Congress Cataloging-in-Publication Data
Moldovo, Eustacia.
 Baby zebras at the zoo / Eustacia Moldovo.
     pages cm. — (All about baby zoo animals)
 Audience: Age 4-6.
 Audience: K to Grade 3.
 Summary: "Describes the life of a zebra foal at a zoo, including its behaviors, diet, and physical traits"—Provided by publisher.
 Includes bibliographical references and index.
 ISBN 978-0-7660-7095-0 (library binding)
 ISBN 978-0-7660-7093-6 (pbk.)
 ISBN 978-0-7660-7094-3 (6-pack)
 1. Zebras—Infancy—Juvenile literature. 2. Zoo animals—Juvenile literature. I. Title.
 QL737.U62M65 2016
 599.665'7139—dc23
                    2015000150

Printed in the United States of America

To Our Readers: We have done our best to make sure all Web sites in this book were active and appropriate when we went to press. However, the author and the publisher have no control over and assume no liability for the material available on those Web sites or on any Web sites they may link to. Any comments or suggestions can be sent by e-mail to customerservice@enslow.com.

Photo Credits: Cbenjasuwan/Shutterstock.com, p. 16; cjorgens/Shutterstock.com, pp. 3 (left), 8; Danny Alvarez/Shutterstock.com, pp. 3 (right), 20; Henk Bentlage/Shutterstock.com, pp. 3 (center), 18; H. van der Winden/Shutterstock.com, p. 1; Johan Swanepoel/Shutterstock.com, p. 14; John Lindsay-Smith/Shutterstock.com, p. 6; Karel Gallas/Shutterstock.com, p. 22; LeonP/Shutterstock.com, p. 10; Peter Erik Forsberg/age footstock/SuperStock, pp. 4–5; Victor Soares/Shutterstock.com, p. 12.

Cover Credits: Johan Swanepoel/Shutterstock.com (zebra foal running); Nelson Marques/Shutterstock.com (baby blocks on spine).

Contents

Words to Know..................... 3

Who Lives at the Zoo?.......... 5

Read More........................... 24

Web Sites............................ 24

Index.................................. 24

Words to Know

foal   grazing   neigh

Who lives at the zoo?

A baby zebra lives at the zoo!

A baby zebra is called a foal.

Zebra foals have brown and white stripes. They turn black and white when they get older.

Each zebra foal has its own special set of stripes. All zebras may look the same, but really they are different.

A zebra foal can stand, walk, and run soon after it is born.

A zebra foal lives with its family at the zoo. A family of zebras is called a harem.

A zebra foal eats grass. Eating grass is called grazing.

A zebra foal neighs like a horse. It also barks and snorts.

You can see a zebra foal at the zoo!

Read More

Meister, Cari. *Zebras*. Minneapolis, Minn.: Bullfrog Books, 2015.

Peterson, Megan Cooley. *Zebras Are Awesome!* Mankato, Minn.: Capstone Press, 2015.

Web Sites

National Geographic Kids: Zebra
kids.nationalgeographic.com/content/kids/en_US/animals/zebra/

San Diego Zoo Kids: Zebra
kids.sandiegozoo.org/animals/mammals/zebra

Index

foal, 9, 11, 13, 15, 17, 19, 21, 23
grass, 19
grazing, 19
harem, 17

neigh, 21
stripes, 11, 13
zoo, 5, 7, 17, 23

Guided Reading Level: D
Guided Reading Leveling System is based on the guidelines recommended by Fountas and Pinnell.

Word Count: 118